Learning Photography

SHOOTING IN MANUAL MODE

DAVID EDWARDS

© Copyright 2020 - All rights reserved.

The content contained within this book may not be reproduced, duplicated or transmitted without direct written permission from the author or the publisher.

Under no circumstances will any blame or legal responsibility be held against the publisher, or author, for any damages, reparation, or monetary loss due to the information contained within this book, either directly or indirectly.

Legal Notice:

This book is copyright protected. It is only for personal use. You cannot amend, distribute, sell, use, quote or paraphrase any part, or the content within this book, without the consent of the author or publisher.

Disclaimer Notice:

Please note the information contained within this document is for educational and entertainment purposes only. All effort has been executed to present accurate, up to date, reliable, complete information. No warranties of any kind are declared or implied. Readers acknowledge that the author is not engaged in the rendering of legal, financial, medical or professional advice. The content within this book has been derived from various sources. Please consult a licensed professional before attempting any techniques outlined in this book.

By reading this document, the reader agrees that under no circumstances is the author responsible for any losses, direct or indirect, that are incurred as a result of the use of the information contained within this document, including, but not limited to, errors, omissions, or inaccuracies.

CONTENTS

Introduction	5
Chapter 1: **Get to Know Your Camera**	6
Chapter 2: **Aperture Science**	13
Chapter 3: **The Power of Shutter Speed**	23
Chapter 4: **ISO Sensitivity**	28
Chapter 5: **What Else Should You Know About Manual Mode?**	32
Chapter 6: **Composition**	40
Conclusion	53
References	54

Introduction

If you want to create interesting photos that will go above Instagram selfies and vacation memories, you need to switch to manual mode. You probably bought your first semi-professional or professional camera, but it looks so complicated. With all the buttons and switches, new cameras might look scary at the beginning.. It's easy to get overwhelmed. Auto mode is the safest bet, and it served you well up until now. If you are wondering why your photos aren't as good as that photographer with a million followers who has the same camera as you, the answer is probably that he is manually adjusting the exposure to get the desired effect.

Auto mode can get you only so far. It is programmed to perfectly expose the photos without minding the depth of field or the shutter speed. It will adjust the exposure parameters on its own, and you are not in control of the photo that's being created. Manual mode is what allows you to be in complete control, and even though it looks complicated, it really isn't. After all, the exposure has only three elements, and you can easily master them.

A good photo is not just a product of manual mode and exposure settings. While aperture, shutter speed, and ISO are crucial elements for any modern camera (even some smartphones allow you to manipulate these parameters), photography is about telling a story. The camera is just your medium, and you are the artist. This is why at the end of this book you will find a chapter that will introduce you to the basic photography composition rules. There are also some tips and tricks there waiting for you that will improve your photography.

CHAPTER 1:
GET TO KNOW YOUR CAMERA

All modern cameras come with pre-programmed modes that are easy to use, and even though they have some advantages, you can only take full control of the camera in manual mode. Shooting with pre-programmed modes is easy. Usually, it means you just point the camera at the desired object and press the button. However, if you want to unlock the full potential of your camera, it's time to switch to M (manual). But shooting in manual mode is not easy, and beginners have a lot to learn before they are able to produce high-quality photos. In manual mode, it is you, the photographer, who has control over all the camera settings. They will determine if the photo will be good or bad, successful, or a total disaster. In order to learn how to control those settings, you need to understand how the camera works and the basic functions you will manipulate in order to take quality photos.

There are different types of cameras out there that are designed to meet the needs of all people interested in photography. The two most popular types today are DSLR and mirrorless cameras. They are both models with interchangeable lenses and are considered professional cameras. DSLR cameras use mirrors which reflect the image from the lens, through the viewfinder, into the eye of the photographer so he can see exactly what the camera sees. Mirrorless, as the name itself suggests, does not have that mirror. Instead, it uses a digital preview of the image you will shoot using an electronic viewfinder. Both types of cameras are capable of producing high-quality images, and it is up to you to decide which one suits you better. Each has its advantages and disadvantages, and both types of cameras come in a variety of designs that will suit beginners or professionals.

How Does a Camera Work?

No matter which type of camera you choose, the secrets of how they turn light into photographs are intriguing. In principle, it is the same as the human eye. The camera needs light in order to see. If you are standing in a room with no windows or source of electrical light, you are in complete darkness and you can't see anything. Just like the eye, the camera's sensor needs a source of light to capture the details. This is why, artistically, photography is also referred to as "painting with light."

When a source of light hits an object in the darkroom you are standing in, it bounces off that object, enabling you to see it. Generally, in nature, light bounces off from all the various objects, and it flows in all directions. Our eyes and the camera lens are able to redirect the light rays which bounce off the objects to a single point. This is how we get a sharp and clear image. The first camera ever made took well over 8 hours to produce a single photo. Imagine how much technology has advanced when now all it takes is a fraction of a second. In order to produce a photo, a modern camera is capable of redirecting the light to the sensor in a very short time. But in order to achieve that sharpness, a photographer needs to know how to adjust the lens properly. This is called focusing. If the focus is neglected, the light will hit the camera's sensor from various directions creating a blurry, out-of-focus photo. Each lens has a focusing system, and it can be either manual, where you need to turn the focusing ring of the lens with your hand until you see a sharp image, or it can be auto-focus, a built-in camera system which will do it for you. No matter if you choose to focus manually, or use the autofocus, the lens will move its glass part further away from or closer to the sensor, allowing you to achieve sharpness.

A camera is able to collect and focus the light to create the image. But how does it record that image? The method differs for digital and film cameras. Film cameras use light-sensitive materials and chemicals. When they are exposed to the light, they capture the shapes and details of an object. Then, the light-sensitive material (film) is taken to the darkroom, where it is exposed to various chemicals that will develop it and create a photo. Digital cameras also capture shapes and details of objects just the same as the film cameras. However, instead of using a light-sensitive material such as film, digital cameras have built-in light sensors. They are divided into a myriad of green, blue, and red pixels. These pixels are gathering the information from the light. The more pixels a sensor has, the higher the quality of the photo because the camera will have more information to work with. The color value of these pixels is what enables the camera's computer to estimate dark and light areas as well as colors and shades. Putting the information gathered from all of the pixels together creates an image.

Besides the number of pixels, another important thing is the size of the sensor. Larger sensors are able to capture more light, and they are perfect for photographing in the low light conditions. If the sensor is small, it needs to be packed with lots of smaller pixels. Because the size matters, smaller pixels cannot store all the available information, and the quality of the photo will be lower.

Why So Many Lenses?

You probably noticed that anyone who uses an SLR camera or even a mirrorless one has more than one lens with them at all times. This is because all the professional and semi-professional cameras have the option to change the lens in order to get different results. There are various types of lenses, and by deciding what you want to shoot, how to achieve a certain composition, or an effect you desire, you will choose a specific lens. Even though there are lenses that can accommodate various needs, such as 15-250 mm, there is a difference between prime, zoom, telephoto, or fish-eye lenses. Photographers are very passionate about their lenses, and they will care more about these accessories than about the camera body itself. This is because the quality of the photo depends on the lens even more than on the camera's sensor.

If you have an entry-level DSLR camera, you will be able to produce photos of higher quality if your lens is good. However, even the most expensive, high-end tech camera will produce bad quality photos if the lens is performing poorly. The lens is the one that will make your camera able to let in the light or to focus. If it's unable to do that properly, there is no camera body in the world that will make a good photograph.

Simply put, a lens is the part of the camera that gathers and focuses the light. The shape of the glass part of the lens will determine in which direction it will focus the light. Lenses are capable of directing the light rays to the exact point on the camera's sensor. This is how the focus is achieved.

Different types of lenses are labeled by numbers and a designation "mm." In order to understand what, for example, an 18-250 mm can achieve, you need to learn how to read the lens symbols. The "mm" designation stands for millimeters and is a measurement for focal length or a distance at which the light rays converge to form a sharp image of an object on the camera's sensor. The focal length of a lens tells us how much of the scene will be captured on a photograph and how much of magnification can be achieved. The smaller the number of focal lengths, more of the scene will be captured. This is called a "wide-angle." The wider the angle, the magnification will be less. This means that an 18 mm lens can capture a wide scene without much magnification. A lens that is 85 mm will capture less scene, but it will magnify the object you are shooting.

If the lens comes with a designation 18-55 mm, it has a focal range of lengths. This lens is called a zoom lens because you can manipulate it and change the focal lens. If the designation is just one number, such as 50 mm, this lens is called a prime lens because it has only one focal length. Both types of lenses have their advantages, and it is up to you to decide which one you will use. However, prime lenses are generally of higher quality because the technology used to make them is simpler, allowing the manufacturers to focus on its quality. This doesn't mean that the zoom lens is useless. In fact, as we learn more, lens technology progresses and makes even zoom lenses high quality.

The advantage of a zoom lens is its versatility. You can manipulate it to shoot different angles and achieve different effects. It can be used in various situations, and it comes in handy when you don't have the time to change the lens (sports events, weddings, concerts, etc.). The advantage of prime lenses is that they come with a larger maximum aperture that allows shooting in low light. Another one is the shallow depth of field, which can create beautiful artistic effects. More on that in later chapters.

The telephoto lens is a lens with a very long focal length. The range can go anywhere from 70 to 600 mm. Telephoto lenses can also be prime or zoom. They are a perfect choice for those photographers whose distance from the object they are shooting is limited; for example, sports photographers or wildlife photographers. However, they are used in portrait or product photography because telephoto lenses will take a photo from a distance and not intrude upon a subject.

The Importance of Exposure

Even though these two types of cameras display the image in different ways through the viewfinder, they work on the same principle. They are equipped with a sensor, which is hit by light in order to produce an image. In M mode a photographer is able to control three main parameters: aperture, shutter speed, and ISO. It is these three parameters that will determine the way the light is hitting the sensor, and how the photo will turn out. The triangle that aperture, shutter speed, and ISO make is called the "Exposure Triangle" because they control the sensor's exposure to light. Mastering these three functions in your camera will give you the opportunity to create photos that always turn out well. They will be of high quality and so much more. By playing with the exposure, you can achieve certain things that will allow you to express yourself through the artistic approach to photography.

In the next chapter, we will talk about each of the exposure parameters—aperture, shutter speed, and ISO—explaining in detail how they work and what you can achieve with them. For now, it is enough if you understand why it is so important to get the exposure right. It is very simple. All photos are made of light and dark areas. If the exposure is done properly, both light and dark areas will be filled with pixels. Pixels are information, and if there are no pixels that means that there is no photo at all. If the sensor of the camera is exposed to too much light (overexposure), you will get light areas that contain no pixels, no information. This is what we call "burned areas" or "blown out areas." The whole image may look too bright, and the details would be invisible. But the burned areas may occur only in some parts of the image, making it difficult to edit.

While the most common error that beginner photographers make is overexposing their photos, there is also a thing called underexposing. It is when not enough light reaches the sensor of the camera. This means that the dark areas will contain no information, and they will turn out too dark. Just as with overexposing, underexposing can influence the whole photo or just some areas, which will be hard to edit because they contain no information to work with. Exposing the photo properly means it's dark and light areas will contain information and the details will be visible.

However, this doesn't mean that overexposing or underexposing is necessarily bad. There are so many things you can achieve if you learn how to control the exposure. Light and dark areas will allow you to express yourself in different ways, and having no detail might be just what a photo needs to give an overall artistic expression. In order to recognize when and what to overexpose or underexpose, you need to perfect the proper exposure.

The manual mode of the camera means you will be given full control over the exposure. Programmed modes let the camera make all the decisions, and the task of the photographer is to point and shoot. All cameras have a built-in light metering system that determines the aperture, shutter speed, and ISO. Even when you switch the camera to manual mode, this metering system continues to work. However, instead of making all the decisions and setting the parameters for itself, the camera will continue to evaluate the light. Through the viewfinder, you will be able to see if the exposure is over, under, or just right.

Then, you as a photographer, need to make the decision which parameters you will change in order to get the desired effect.

If the auto mode is so good at determining the exposure, why would you ever change to manual mode? This is because the auto mode is designed to make all the parts of the photo correctly exposed. But what happens if you want to achieve something different? There are different kinds of effects you can get by having full control over the aperture, shutter speed, and ISO. For example, you want to take a photo of a silhouette. With auto mode, this would be impossible because the camera would constantly try to correct the dark, underexposed areas even if you want them hidden in shadows. This is why you need to take full control of your camera.

CHAPTER 2:
APERTURE SCIENCE

Aperture is one of the three parameters you can manipulate in order to set the desired exposure in your camera. However, the aperture is actually a part of the lens, not the body of the camera. Every lens has it. It is the "pupil" of the camera through which the light passes. Just as with the pupil of the human eye, the aperture can expand to let in more light or shrink to limit the amount of light reaching the sensor. The more you open the aperture, the less light will be needed to expose the photo.

Aperture has another very important purpose. It can manipulate the depth of field (DOF), meaning that the parts that are not focused seem blurred. They can be either background (everything behind the focused object) or the foreground (everything in front of the focused object). Manipulating depth of field allows you to be very creative with your photos, but sometimes it can be a bad thing. For example, shallow depth of field is undesired in landscape photography where everything needs to be in focus.

Understand the Depth of Field

Because of the effect that shallow depth of field creates, many photographers prioritize aperture when setting the exposure. They will set the aperture to create the desired effect and continue manipulating shutter speed and ISO in order to get the correct exposure. A large aperture will create a shallow depth of field effect while a small one will have the opposite effect. The depth of field plays the role of bringing the viewers' attention to the main subject of the photograph. It is commonly used in portrait photography where a person is focused while the background is blurred. However, it is often used in fine art photography as it can allow the artist to express his ideas or feelings.

The depth of field depends on so much more than just the aperture. One is the subject's **distance** from the background. If you are photographing a person and he is leaning on the wall behind him, you will not get a blurred background. This is because the distance between the subject and the background is almost nonexistent, so there is no depth to the photo. The more you move your subject away from the background, the greater the blur will be. Another important thing is the distance between the camera and the subject you are shooting. The closer you are to the person, the smaller the depth of field. In other words, taking a close up photo of a flower or even the face of a person with a small aperture will result in parts of the subject being out of focus.

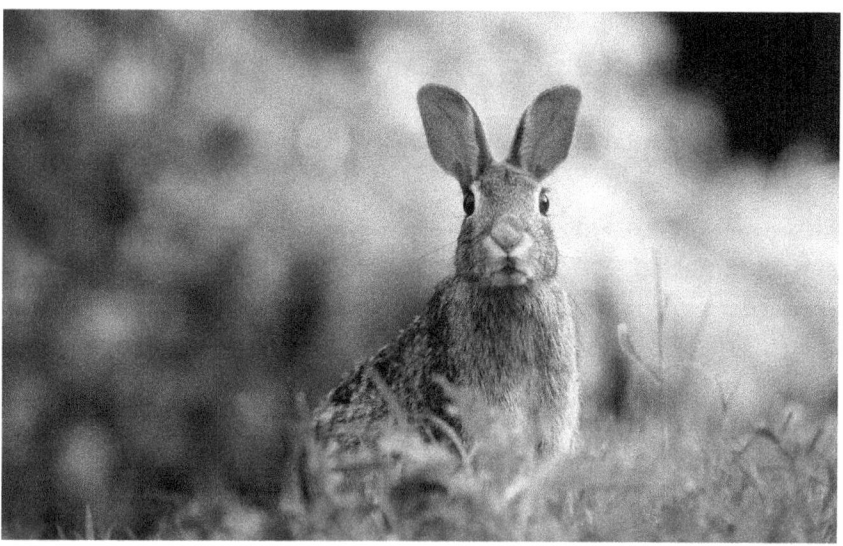

(Photo 1. Example of shallow depth of field, which blurred both the background and foreground, while the focused subject, the rabbit, is sharp and clear.)

The depth of field may be influenced by the **focal length** of the lens you are using. This has something to do with the distance of the camera from the subject that needs to be in focus. If that distance is the same, a wide-angle lens will have a deeper depth of field, while a narrow-angle lens will have a shallower DOF. This means that a photo taken with a 70 mm lens will be sharper than the one taken with a 105 mm lens. But it's not really fair to compare the photos taken with different focal lengths if the distance between the camera and object doesn't change. What creates the effect of shallow depth of field, in this case, is the narrow field of view that 105 mm creates.

If you adjust the distance between the camera and the object that needs to be in focus so that both focal lengths have the same or at least similar fields of view, the DOF will be exactly the same. However, there will be an illusion that a lens with a long focal length creates more blur in the background. This is because of the magnification abilities of the lens. The background will be magnified and less of it will fill the frame, giving the impression it has more blur when in fact it doesn't.

Sensor size also influences the depth of field. Generally speaking, the smaller the sensor, the larger the depth of field. Full frame cameras have larger sensors that will give the effect of a shallower depth of field. This is why portrait and product photographers love using full-frame cameras. But to a beginner, the difference is not that significant, and it can even be manipulated. Just as with focal length and DOF, if you adjust the distance between the camera and the subject, you will get the same result with a DX camera.

There are various formulas and online calculators for the depth of field that can help you calculate it properly based on the gear you own. However, the depth of field should be used creatively and freely. It is enough to know how to achieve shallow or deep DOF. Today, when almost all cameras are digital, you have the option of previewing your photos. Most of the cameras have a DOF preview button that will show you through the viewfinder what the end result of the photo you are taking will be before you shoot it. If you are using a live view, remember that you don't need to press the DOF preview button because the screen always shows what the photo will look like once you take it. If your camera doesn't have it, use an LCD screen to preview the image you just took and decide if you want to give it another go with different camera settings.

What Is an F-stop?

We already said that aperture can be large or small, fully opened or closed. In photography, the size of the opening of aperture is described as an f-stop or the f-number. Whenever you change the size of the aperture's opening, the camera will show you at what f-stop you are. All lenses come with the f-stop designation, and cameras will register your aperture setting and show you its numeric value. You must have seen that your camera is displaying something like f/2.8 or f/5.6 or even f/12. Some cameras display it without a slash as f2.8 or f11.

What does that "f" actually stand for? How do we measure the aperture? F stands for focal lengths, and the aperture is measured in fractions. The focal lengths are substituted into a fraction to get the diameter of the opening of the blades which construct the aperture. The mathematics behind it isn't really necessary for taking good photos, but it doesn't hurt to understand how aperture works. It can only help you expand your knowledge and make photographic decisions easier. Let's say that you have a lens with a focal length range 80-200 mm f/2.8. When it is fully zoomed out on 80 mm and the aperture is set to f/4, that means that 80mm/4 equals 20. The diameter of the aperture blades in your lens is 20 mm.

Remember we said aperture is measured in fractions? In that case, the designation f/8 is a fraction and can be written as ⅛ (one-eighth). As a result, the smaller the number, the larger the aperture. To visualize it and remember it more easily, think of the glass half-filled with water. One half is more water than one-eighth, right? Using the same principle of fractions f/2 is larger than f/8.

Remember that the lenses usually come with the f-stop numbers written on them. This is because they need to mark the maximum and minimum opening of the aperture that a specific lens is capable of. You can't set just any number. If a lens has a designation f/4, you won't be able to open it to f/2. This is because the blades of the aperture can only open and close to a certain point. However, the more blades a lens has, the wider it will open. Lenses with large aperture designations are very popular, and you can find some amazing products with the designations f/1.8 or even f/1.4. This is because they are capable of letting more light hit the sensor and are amazing for working in low light conditions. Another reason is the depth of field. The larger the aperture, the more blurry the background. Large apertures and wide angles are extremely popular in astrophotography because the maximum opening of the blades will allow the light to hit the sensor enough to take the image of the sky with stars.

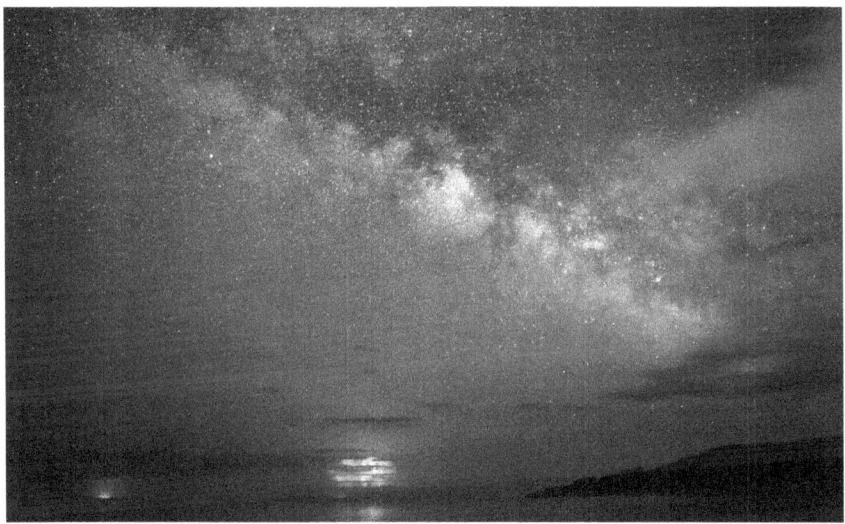

(Photo 2. This photo was taken with an aperture of f/1.8. However, there are more techniques to astrophotography worth discovering.)

Diffraction and Aberration

When it comes to photography mistakes, most of them are caused by the photographer's poor decisions, such as overexposure, poor composition, too much editing, etc. However, there are a few mistakes that happen due to lens design. This doesn't mean that photographers cannot influence them. It just means that there is no such thing as a perfect lens. Designing lenses is a difficult job. To overcome one problem, another will appear. The laws of physics limit the manufacturing of lenses, and it is physically impossible to make them without flaws. This is why some apertures cannot go beyond certain numbers. They are physically unable to open or close more. The other problem is the shape of the glass used to create the lens.

Knowing how to recognize the lens problems will make it easier to deal with them. There are two major problems encountered with the lenses. One is the effect of the **diffraction**. It is a common problem that occurs with small aperture values such as f/16, f/22, and everything beyond. Those of you who studied physics are probably familiar with the term "diffraction," but the majority of people have never heard of it. This problem occurs when the aperture is so small that the light rays reaching the sensor start interfering with each other. Because a small aperture is squeezing the light rays through the tiny hole, their trajectory is changed and they cross each other's path. This results in the image being blurry.

Remember in the previous section we said that smaller apertures are ideal for landscape photographers? This is because of the deeper depth of field that will result in an image with all its parts equally sharp. Naturally, this leads to the conclusion that the smaller the f-stop, the clearer and sharper the photograph will be. But that is not always the case. At some point, the aperture opening will be too small, and it will cause diffraction resulting in a blurry image. The lenses come with the ability to close the aperture to small f-stops, but it is up to the photographer to decide when to stop closing it.

All lenses are different, and the designers are constantly trying to find a way to deal with the diffraction. Some lenses show the first signs of the problem at f/8 or f/11. However, they might be insignificant and won't influence the photo as the artistic expression. But when you close the aperture to f/22 or anything beyond that, the quality drastically falls, and both photographers and observers are bothered by the blurry end result. The diffraction shouldn't be avoided at all costs. If it's insignificant and barely visible, it is worth allowing it to happen in order to get the desired depth of field. Be brave and experiment shooting with f/11 and f/16; see the results for yourself and decide if the results are satisfying.

Another problem is lens **aberrations** (distortions and errors), and although it is completely the fault of the lens design, it is possible to minimize its effects through the right usage of aperture. Aberrations occur due to various lens design flaws, and it can cause different effects. Some of them are blurs in unwanted areas, vignetting, color fringing, or the curvature of the field. There are many aberrations, and it would take a whole new chapter to talk about them in detail. But the most important thing about the aberrations is how you can use aperture to avoid them.

Aberrations often happen when the aperture is opened wide like when you set the large f-stop to f/1.4 or f/1.8. Because aperture blocks the light coming from the edges of the lens, it is able to narrow the beam hitting the sensor. When there is nothing to narrow that beam, as in the aperture is wide open and nothing is blocking the light, the image loses its sharpness. This means that an image taken with f/1.4 will look blurry compared to the image taken with f/5.6. Even though the light is partially blocked and it doesn't come from the edge of the lens, the photons will still cover the entire sensor. You can even try this on your own eye. If you look through a tube, even if it doesn't have a glass at the end, your view will seem sharper than without the tube. This is because the tube is narrowing the light beam entering your eye, making the picture clearer.

Taking into consideration that aberrations happen with the aperture wide open and that the diffractions happen when the aperture is closed, the midpoint will give you the perfect quality of a photo. This means that most lenses produce the sharpest images in the range between f/4 and f/8. However, this doesn't mean you should sacrifice depth of field caused by the aperture in order to get sharper images. Sometimes, it is worth sacrificing a bit of quality for art.

What's *Bokeh*?

Bokeh, or sometimes Boke, is a Japanese word that translates to *blur*. However, not all blurs are bokeh. Bokeh is desired, and all the blurs that are errors are simply that, errors. The photography term "Bokeh" actually represents the quality of the desired blur. If we use a shallow depth of field to create the blurry background which successfully separates the objects, this is called "background blur." However, the impression this blur makes on the viewer as well as its quality in terms of how it reflects the points of light is what we refer to as bokeh.

While some photographers argue that only the circular light reflections caused by the lens are what bokeh is about, the general opinion is that the quality of the whole blurred area matters, not just the highlights. Because of this, photographers denote the difference between types of bokeh such as smooth, silky, soft, or geometrical.

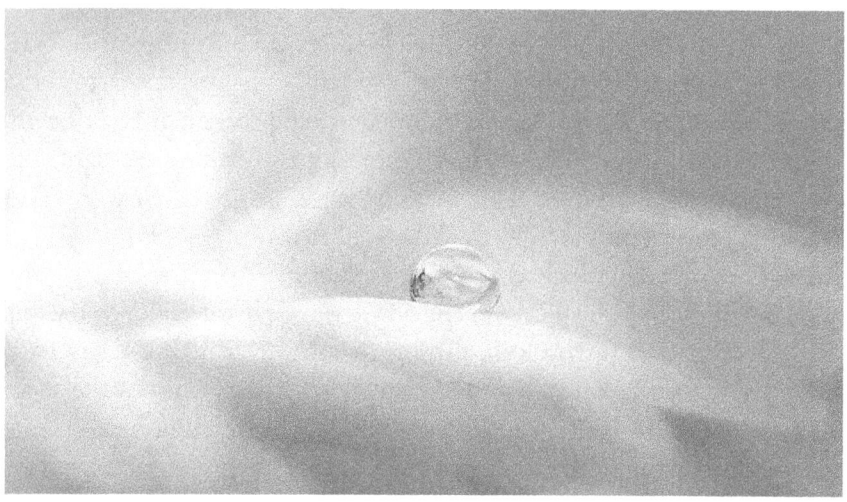

(Photo 3. Silky bokeh without geometrical highlights caused by the lens.)

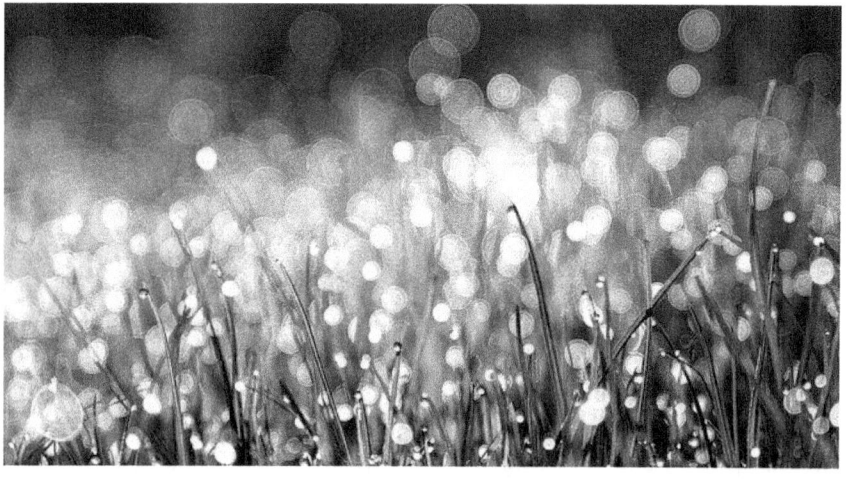

(Photo 4. Geometrical, circular bokeh caused by the light reflections and large aperture.)

Looking at the photos above, the difference between the types of bokeh is obvious. It is not just the circular effect of how the lens renders the light reflections that makes a bokeh. All intentionally blurred parts of a photograph have a certain quality, and it is this quality that makes up the bokeh. It is important to understand the difference between good and bad bokeh.

Because of the unique optical designs and abilities of various lenses, the bokeh will look different depending on which one are you using. The quality of the lens plays a huge role in creating good or bad bokeh. Generally speaking, good portrait and telephoto lenses usually make more appealing bokeh, while low quality consumer lenses do not. However, there are some lenses that are cheap but have a unique design flaw which creates interesting bokeh effects. For example, the Helios 44-2 58 mm f/2.0 creates an interesting swirly bokeh that creates a whirlpool around the subject.

So what is the difference between a good and bad bokeh? Simply said, the good bokeh is the one that pleases the eye. It is smooth, silky, and soft. It gives the impression that an object is in a dreamy, magical place. Bad bokeh is the one that is distracting. The focus needs to be on the object, and if there are too many sharp elements that distract our view and lead the attention away from the object, that is a bad bokeh. However, some photographers argue that there is no such thing as a bad bokeh, and they might be right. In the end, it all depends on the intention of a photographer and what he was trying to show through a photo.

To get good bokeh, there are some rules a photographer needs to follow. Bokeh is achieved with a shallow depth of field, and this means not just using the bigger aperture. Of course, the aperture matters, but as we explained earlier, if there is no distance between the object and the background, you won't be able to achieve a shallow depth of field. Another requirement for a good bokeh is that a photographer needs to be at the same level as the object in focus. If you are shooting from above, then there is not enough light reflection to cause the bokeh. If you are shooting from below, there will probably be too much light as the sun will hit the lens directly. Another important thing is that the background needs to be interesting, colorful, and even have multiple small sources of light or light reflecting surfaces behind the subject. Try experimenting with Christmas lights or aluminum foil as the background. In nature, it is quite easy to find colorful backgrounds. Just look around and see the various leaves of a tree or a complex of buildings in the distance whose windows will reflect the light perfectly.

Prime lenses are usually of higher quality, and they will produce magnificent bokeh. They also have the ability to set the aperture to a very low number such as f/1.4. These are needed for a shallow depth of field. However, high-end quality telephoto and zoom lenses are capable of producing beautiful bokeh too. The shape of the rendered light reflection can vary from a smooth circle to those with edges. This is caused by the number of blades in the aperture. The larger the number, the smoother the aperture will open, leaving perfect circles. A small number of blades makes it impossible for the aperture to open as a perfect circle. Instead, it will render the reflection as a hectagon, for example; but even this can be smoothed out to a perfect circle with the shallow depth of field, using very large aperture openings such as f/1.4 or f/1.8.

Bokeh is very pleasing to the eye, and if it's not distracting, it will focus on the desired object even more by bringing the viewer's attention to it. However, this doesn't mean you should strive to achieve the bokeh at all times. Sometimes, it is undesired and unwanted. There is even a complaint in the photography circles that bokeh is overused and that there is too much emphasis on it. Bokeh, as an element of the photograph, needs to serve a purpose and tell the story. More about bokeh in the chapter about photo composition.

CHAPTER 3:
THE POWER OF SHUTTER SPEED

The second most important setting of the exposure triangle is shutter speed. Every camera has a curtain in front of the sensor which is closed when the camera is resting. However, as soon as you press the button to shoot, that curtain (shutter) opens to allow the sensor to be exposed to the light coming through the lens. Once the sensor is done collecting the light, the shutter will close to stop extra light from hitting the sensor. This is precisely why the button that controls the shutter is also called the shutter, or shutter button. It is the same button that focuses the camera, allowing you to take the photograph.

Shutter speed is nothing else but the length of time for which the curtain remains open. It is how long the sensor is exposed to the light or how long it takes to complete the photo. The purpose of the shutter speed is to manipulate exposure, but it also creates two very different and desired effects. It can freeze the motion or action, or it can blur the motion creating the sense of movement.

Long shutter speed is when you expose the sensor to the light over a significant period of time. The longer the exposure, the more blurred the action you are capturing will be. Moving subjects, such as cars or people, will be influenced by this effect, while the still objects, such as buildings, will not. This blurring effect gives a sense of motion, speed, and movement of the objects. It is often used in commercial photography to emphasize the speed of a car or a motorcycle. But it can also be used creatively to express motion through the artist's view. A dancer captured with slow shutter speed would look ethereal, light, and magnificently elegant while showing all his moves.

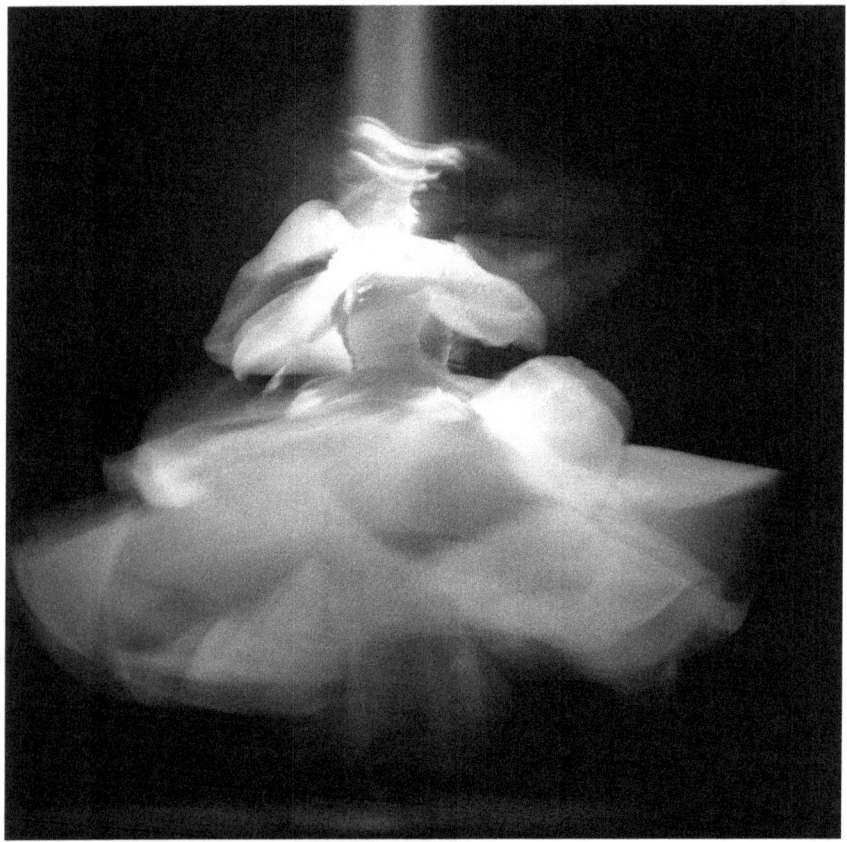

(Photo 5. Example of a dancer taken with a slow shutter speed, therefore a long exposure.)

The opposite of a long exposure is the short one. It is when the camera's sensor is exposed to the light for a fraction of time. With the fast shutter speed, you will get the opposite effect, and you will be able to freeze the motion. The most common use of fast shutter speed is when photographing children, animals, and wildlife in general, sports events, and so on. A dancer caught with the fast shutter speed would be sharper, and the details would be more visible.

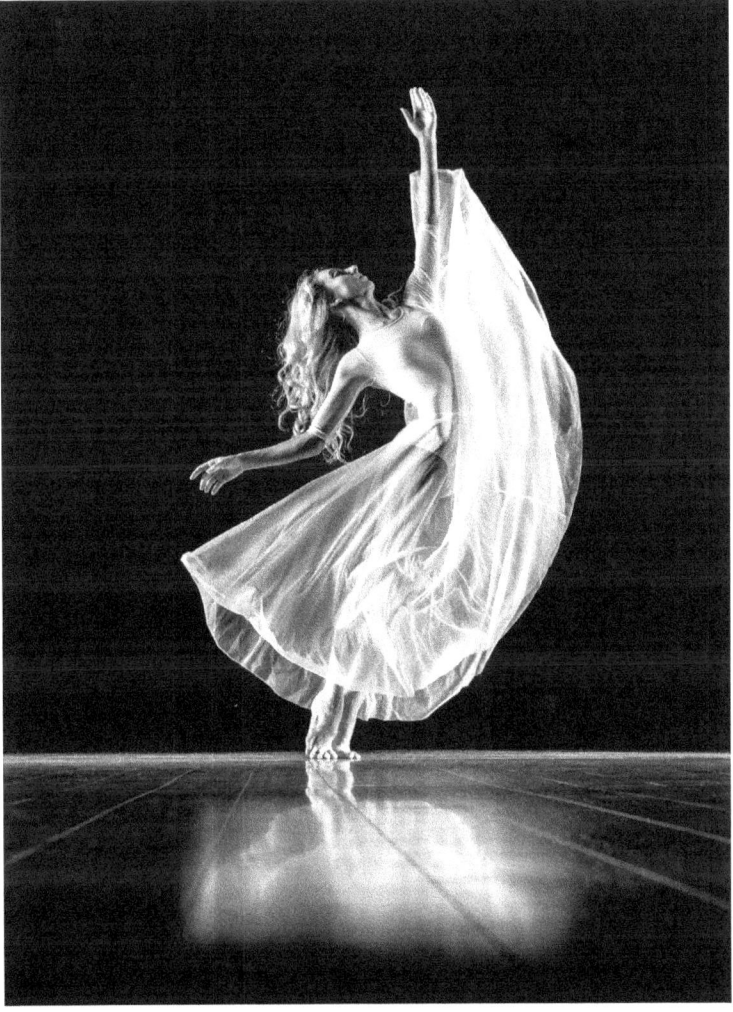

(Photo 6. A dancer photographed with a fast shutter speed, therefore a short exposure.)

The Importance of Shutter Speed

Before understanding how to control the exposure by using shutter speed, you will need to get acquainted with how it is measured. Quite simply, the measurement for shutter speed is time. However, it all happens so quickly that we are talking about a fraction of a second. The camera will show your shutter speed setting as a number, for example, 1/20. This means that once you press the shutter button, it will stay open for one-twentieth of a second. In terms of photography, 1/20 is very slow and if you are holding the camera with your hands, any slight movement will influence the photo and it will be blurred. We are all constantly in movement, and there is no such thing as completely steady hands capable of handling long exposure. The solution is to use a tripod which will stabilize the camera.

However, long exposures can go over a full second, even for hours if we allow it to and if the camera is capable of shooting for so long. The problem with long exposures is that the camera can heat up pretty quickly and break down. This is why if you choose to shoot over a long period of time, with the extremely long exposure you will need to take the temperature of your surroundings into account.

Remember that the shutter speed also influences the exposure. If you are using long exposure, the photos can get very bright. And if you are using short exposure, the photos might turn out very dark. To get the perfect exposure, you need to manipulate all three parameters—aperture, shutter speed, and ISO—to get the desired brightness of the photo. This means that if you want to shoot long exposure, you will have to adjust it first, and then manipulate aperture and ISO until the balanced exposure is achieved.

Remember that long exposure means that the sensor is exposed to the light for a longer time. This means that on a sunny day, you do not want to shoot with long exposure. It will definitely result in overexposed photos unless you use specially designed filters that would allow you to set a long exposure even with plenty of light. These filters are called neutral-density filters, or short ND. Long exposures typically start at one second, but everything between 1/100 and one second is considered too slow for you to hand hold your camera. Our hands shake whether we notice it or not, and the camera is sensitive enough to register those shapes and record them. The end result will be a blurry image. Luckily, modern lenses are equipped with an image stabilization system (vibration reduction) that allows you to hold your camera even at 1/60 second. Remember that given numbers are average, and they can vary from individual to individual. Experiment with your camera, and find the optimal shutter speed that suits your needs.

CHAPTER 4:
ISO SENSITIVITY

The last piece of the exposure triangle is ISO or "International Organization for Standardization." Yes, it is confusing that a camera setting is connected to an organization. Well, in reality, it isn't. The term is borrowed from the light sensitivity standards of camera films issued in the 1970s. Even though the film standards are not the same as the digital ISO, they are both about light sensitivity. While the ISO began as the standard of film's sensitivity to light, for digital cameras it stands for the sensor's sensitivity to the light. But film and sensors are not the same things, and they do work on different principals. Therefore, the ISO standard for the film is not the same as the ISO standard for the camera sensor. The technical term for digital cameras is actually "Exposure index," but since the ISO has been used for so long, it became a standard name for measuring light sensitivity.

ISO is what a camera can do to digitally brighten your photo. It has values that determine how much exposure will be added. Common values are ISO 100, ISO 200, ISO 400, ISO 800, ISO 1600, ISO 3200, and ISO 6400. Doubling the ISO means you are adding double the brightness to the photo. There are other ISO values other than the mentioned standards, but they will significantly influence the quality of the image by adding digital noise.

Every camera has a base ISO value, which is also the lowest. You should strive to shoot with the base value whenever it is possible. This is because it will guarantee that there is no digital noise to lower the quality of the photo. When working in low light conditions, you will have to increase your ISO in order to keep aperture and shutter speed at their best for the desired effects. Modern cameras have ISO values which can go very high, even above 12,000. But these high ISO are to be avoided because the quality of the photo will be significantly lower.

Every camera is different, and the digital noise starts appearing at different ISO values. Experiment with your camera, and find where that value is for your camera. Usually, the LCD screen on your device is too small to notice digital noise, and it may trick you and encourage you to go high with ISO. But if you enlarge the image, you will easily see how the ISO influences the quality, even directly, from the camera's LCD screen.

How and When to Change ISO Settings

Modern digital cameras always have a shortcut through which you can access the ISO setting and quickly change it. However, some older and some mirrorless cameras can access ISO only through the menu. Check your camera manual if you are not sure where the button for manipulating ISO values is. The ISO button is often used, and that is why camera designers are trying to make it as available as possible.

Now that you understand how the ISO works, it's time to learn how to properly use it. ISO affects the brightness of the photo, but it also allows you to get creative with aperture and shutter speed. We already mentioned that because of the digital noise that appears at the high ISO, you should always strive to use it at the base value. But in many situations, it won't be possible to use the lowest value. This is why it is important to know exactly when the noise appears.

Digital noise is dots of green, blue, or red added to the photo by your camera. It is completely different from the film grain that appears due to chemical reactions and adds texture to the photo. Digital noise is a defect, and while film grain is color neutral, the noise isn't and it is often seen as colored pixels (especially noticeable in blue colored areas). Another difference is that the grain can be of various sizes. It depends on the sensitivity of the film, but the digital noise always takes the space of one pixel. That one pixel is destroyed and unusable because it contains false information.

One of the interesting facts about digital photography is that you can use high ISO values if you have enough light to shoot with low ISO. The noise will still be there, but it will be less noticeable. This is because if you have enough light, the areas covered in shadow will be smaller. The noise is most visible in the areas covered in shadow. Low light ambients are filled with deep shadows and are perfect for displaying noise.

When to Use Low ISO

Low ISO is commonly used when there is enough light to comfortably shoot with whatever aperture and shutter speed settings you want. If you use a tripod or keep your camera completely still on a table or any other firm surface, you will also be able to use low ISO even if the light is dim. In that case, to keep the ISO at a minimum, you will have to compensate with long shutter speed or wide open aperture. This will influence the depth of field and the appearance of movement trails. If this effect is not desired at the moment of shooting, you will have to raise the ISO values.

Let's say you want to take a photo of car light trails during the night. In that case, you will shoot with a very long exposure. To keep the depth of field optimal, you cannot open your aperture otherwise the car lights will be out of focus in the distance. Try shooting with a long exposure that is well over a second long. Try setting it to 15 seconds. Keep your aperture closed, at least to f/11. In this case, your ISO value can be at a minimum because the length of shutter speed compensates for the brightness.

When to Use High ISO

There are plenty of opportunities to use high ISO values, even though the recommendation is to stick to the base one. High ISO is necessary when you want to fight the motion blur. Shooting fast-moving objects often means you will have to shoot with fast shutter speed.

The bad way to approach this problem is to open up your aperture. This way you will run the risk of losing the sharpness of the photo. Instead, keep your aperture optimal to give you the best results and try raising your ISO. If you are shooting during the day, it's even better because the noise caused by high ISO won't be as visible.

High ISO is commonly used by wildlife photographers who are experts at freezing the movement of animals. Photographing birds is a good way to practice this, especially seagulls who are often flying over the water and are easy to follow with your camera. To capture the movement of a bird, you will often have to shoot at incredible speed, even as high as 1/4000 of a second (though it would rarely need to go that high). Even on a sunny day, if you are shooting that fast, you will need to raise the ISO to approximately 800. Keep in mind that given values are just an example, and they will vary just as the light conditions vary.

Simply put, you shouldn't be afraid to raise the ISO when the situation demands it. Your photos still need to be sharp and bright, and because of it, the aperture and shutter speed will determine what ISO value is needed. If you are having trouble with ISO and noise, consider using flash or any other external light source. It will help you lower the ISO values if needed. But don't be afraid to experiment. If the photo captures an amazing story, the appearance of digital noise rarely lowers the quality.

CHAPTER 5:
WHAT ELSE SHOULD YOU KNOW ABOUT MANUAL MODE?

Now that you know what each of the camera settings is capable of, you can start playing with your camera like a professional and switch it to manual mode. As a beginner, you are probably already familiar with "point and shoot" tactics. It is what smartphones are doing, and there are even consumer class "point and shoot" cameras designed specifically for that. With the development of technology, even our smartphones are capable of producing amazing photos. So why should you bother to switch to manual mode? There are several very good reasons.

First, and maybe the most important reason is that you will have complete control over your camera. Yes, exposure is important, but the manual mode will allow you to do so much more. You will be able to set the desired focus point or switch to complete manual focus. You can choose the way your camera meters the light or how it adjusts the white balance. In the end, controlling all the exposure elements will give you artistic freedom. In auto mode, the camera does everything for you, and you are just there to press the button. In manual mode, you need to think about setting each exposure parameter separately in order to get the desired effect. If you allow the camera to make all the decisions, you are only there for the ride, and most of the time, you won't be truly pleased with your photos.

Another very good reason to switch to manual mode is artistic freedom. By making your own decisions and setting the aperture, shutter speed, and ISO, you will be able to achieve various effects. Auto mode won't allow you this freedom. If the camera makes all the decisions, you can't control depth of field or exposure time. Maybe you will want to purposely underexpose a photo or overexpose it. This is often done by artists who use exposure mistakes on purpose to express themselves and achieve stunning results. The camera is programmed to do everything perfectly, even if it means taking uninteresting photos.

Shooting in manual mode requires practice. You can read all the information about exposure that is available to you and still make very bad photos if you have no practice. This is because it will take some time for you to get used to the camera. It will also take some time to learn how to think ahead and correctly set all the parameters. Many beginners dislike manual mode because they think that setting the aperture, shutter speed, and ISO takes time, and the moment you wanted to photograph may pass before your camera is ready. This is true to a point. However, if you are out there shooting multiple shots during one session, chances are you will have to set your camera only once and adjust one or two of the exposure elements every now and then. With practice, this takes no time at all. When you get to know your camera, your fingers will work automatically, and you won't even need to put it down and look at which buttons you are pressing. Practice will make it truly easy and satisfactory.

If you still feel uncomfortable switching from auto to manual mode, try moving up slowly and shooting in aperture mode (usually designated with an A on the camera). Aperture mode is a compromise between auto and manual modes. This will give you full control over the aperture and ISO while the camera will automatically set shutter speed to compensate. You can choose to keep ISO at the base value if the light is plentiful, or you can set it to a higher level if there is not enough light. This way, you can practice the depth of field and understand it completely. You can get very creative in this mode, and there are even situations where it is better than the manual mode; for example, if the light conditions are changing very quickly or you simply don't have the time to play with all the settings.

Shoot RAW

Digital cameras and smartphones are set to shoot in JPEG or JPG format by default. These two are different abbreviations for the same format of images. It stands for "Joint Photographic Experts Group," and it is a standardized format which can be viewed using almost all devices out there. This is possible because JPEG is a compressed file format. If you shoot in JPEG format, the camera will apply various optimizations to the photo in order to make the file smaller in size. The small size also means less information. Because of this loss of information, the quality of the photo will suffer. The bigger the compression, the less quality an image will have. But small file size means it needs less storage space. This is why JPEG is good when it comes to uploading and displaying your photos online.

The downside of JPEG is the lack of information. This is because the compression process discards all the extra image data which would be used in photo editing. The lost information cannot be returned, and while editing, you simply have less to work with. Another problem is that during the compression process, the camera adjusts the contrast, sharpness, and saturation. Even though you are still able to change these in editing programs, you will never be able to start from the beginning and work with the original information. This will result in unsatisfactory photos.

This is why professionals choose to shoot in RAW file formats. Even though you will encounter RAW written capitalized, remember that RAW is not actually a file format. It can also be written lowercase, "raw," because that is what it means. It is the unedited and uncompressed file of various formats. In fact, each camera has its own file extension for raw images such as Nikon's NEF or Canon's CR2. Most of the time photographers capitalize RAW simply out of habit. Most of the new photographers don't even realize that raw is not an extension but a word to describe an unprocessed file. As food can be raw and needs preparation and cooking, photographs need preparation or processing, and that is why we call them raw files.

There is no rule that says you have to shoot in raw. However, the advantages of raw make a great difference. All the image data will be contained ensuring high quality. If you got your exposure right and the sky turned out too dark (not at all how you saw it), it is not the end. The information of all the colors in the sky are there in the raw photo. All you have to do is retrieve it. Editing programs have a set of tools that will help you do that. You can lower the highlights of the sky and increase shadows to get a more dramatic look of the sky. This is not "repainting" the photo. All the information is already there, and all you are doing is bringing it out, making it visible.

Another advantage of shooting raw has nothing to do with editing the photos later on your computer. It is all about how the camera manages the white balance. If you are shooting JPEG, you won't have control over the white balance. The camera will decide how to render the light's color and how to display it in the photo. This can turn out poorly as a camera is a machine and it doesn't have a human's ability to perceive aesthetics. Sometimes, it will get the exact white balance you want, but most of the time it will miss and all the photos will look unnatural. Shooting in raw gives you the opportunity to decide whatever white balance setting you want.

Remember that raw photos don't look as good as JPEG. They tend to appear as if the colors are washed up. This happens because JPEG is an already edited photo, and the editing was done inside the camera by applying a certain camera profile to the photo. You, as the photographer, have no control over this editing. It is programmed and done by the camera. It might give the impression that the camera is doing better in JPEG than in raw, but it's all about the possibilities. With JPEG, you can make fewer changes, but you won't be able to edit the photo the way you want. Raw can be manipulated in more ways, and you can achieve the JPEG look or go for something completely different. You have all the information available in raw photos; you just need to bring it out on the surface.

The last important thing to remember about the raw files is that you cannot upload them to social media as they are, in their original file extensions, and not all photo viewing programs will be able to open your raw photos. They have to be processed and compressed into JPEG, or whatever standardized file extension you prefer. This is usually done by editing programs such as Photoshop or Lightroom. There, you can even control the compression of the files and decide on the physical and data size of your photos.

Use the Histogram

One of the biggest advantages of shooting in manual mode is the use of histograms. It is a graphical representation of the pixels, and if you learn how to read it, it will help you get the exposure just right. Histograms can be set as a continuous display on the camera's LCD screen, or it can be read later, at any point in time, to analyze the photo. Each photo has its own histogram, and you can access it whenever you want, from the camera or from your preferable editing program.

To read histograms, you need to know that the left side of the graph represents the shadows or the blacks on the photo (value = 0), while the right side represents the whites, or highlights (value = 255). Everything in the middle section is mid-tones. The various peaks in the graph represent the number of pixels for certain tones. The tones between 0 and 255 are each exactly one pixel wide.

A properly exposed photo will have a histogram with a curve reaching from one edge to another, without leaving empty spaces on any of the sides. The curve shouldn't lean heavily on either of the histogram's sides. The middle arch should be perfectly curved reaching the top in the middle and then gently going down. However, not all histograms should be perfect. Sometimes, depending on what a photographer wants to achieve, the histogram can look completely different. The histogram will depend on whether the subject you are shooting is dark or light. For example, if you are shooting a white cat in a well-lit environment, the histogram will show the shift towards the highlights to the right side. If you are shooting a dark object in dim light, the histogram will lean towards the shadows, the left side.

It is not necessary to keep the histogram on while shooting, and as you get better with your photography, you will find that you are capable of making a good decision without looking at it. However, as a beginner, the histogram can give you valuable information. You can pinpoint your mistakes by analyzing the histogram, and you can see if in some areas of the photo the data is lost due to over- or underexposure. If the histogram is showing a sudden spike in either the left or right area, that means that data is lost. The areas affected by data loss are called "clipping areas." Remember that clipping doesn't necessarily mean bad photos. Maybe a photographer did it on purpose to emphasize the darkness or the light. The creative usage of underexposure or overexposure happens a lot.

Light Metering

Modern cameras have a built-in system known as light metering or exposure metering. There are different types of metering modes available, and knowing how each of them works will help you determine what to use. Some of these are essential if you are working in unusual lighting conditions such as concerts or theatres.

Metering is the way your camera measures the light in order to determine the correct exposure. Because of metering, the camera is able to determine if the settings for aperture, shutter speed, and ISO are right. The light meter is a sensor that will measure the intensity of the light as soon as you half-press the shutter button. (Note: pressing the button to only half, without taking a photo, will also focus the area you are pointing at if the autofocus option is selected.)

All DSLR cameras are equipped with the sensor that is capable of measuring the light intensity, but depending on the camera's brand and model, some have slightly different metering modes. However, the main three modes are always the same:

1. Matrix Metering (known as Evaluative Metering on Canon cameras)

2. Center-weighted Metering

3. Spot Metering

The metering bar is what you want to look at to determine what parameters to change in order to get the proper exposure. The bar can be easily seen through the viewfinder, on the LCD screen; or if your camera has a second smaller screen that contains all the setting data, you will find the metering bar there too. It looks like a bar with arrows pointing left or right and with a 0 in the middle. If the arrow is pointing to the left, it will have the designation - (minus) as you are underexposing your photo. If the arrow is showing to the right, it will have the designation + (plus), and it means you are overexposing your photo. You need to set your camera to show 0 (zero) in the middle with no arrows on the sides. This means the exposure is just right. Don't forget to point the camera at the object you plan to shoot while observing the metering bar.

Matrix metering is a default for most cameras. It divides the whole frame into zones, which are then analyzed individually. The light and dark tones are what determine the exposure. However, the metering will prioritize the zone, which is focused on the camera, and determine the correct exposure appropriately. Matrix metering is often used for landscape photography because it covers the whole frame. However, many photographers prefer to use it for portrait or product photography.

Center-weighted metering evaluates the light in the middle of the frame and sets the exposure bar accordingly. This is very handy when you are, for example, taking a portrait of a person with the sun behind his head. This way, the camera will now ignore the light areas around the center and calculate the exposure on the face (provided you are focusing on the face of a person). This mode is perfect for close up shots or whenever you need the object in the middle to have the best possible exposure.

Spot metering evaluates the light only around the focus point. It will ignore everything else. Spot metering is very popular with fine art photographers. It is good to use when you are focusing on a small object (such as birds), especially if they are in the corners of the frame. This way, you will be able to measure the light at any point of the whole frame. Spot metering is also good for portrait photography, as you can easily measure the light on the brightest part of the person and get the skin tones just right. If you like doing portraits, remember to always focus on the eye that is closest to the camera. To measure the light, do not use the eye but the skin just below it. Before shooting, press the shutter button halfway while focusing on the skin just below the eye. Set the exposure to meet the camera's needs, and then focus on the eye and shoot without correcting the exposure. This way, you will get perfect skin tones. Even if the eyes end up a little bit darker (usually they won't), you can always lift the shadows in the editing part.

CHAPTER 6:
COMPOSITION

Photography is about much more than just pointing your camera and shooting. If you want to go beyond selfies and generic vacation photos, you will also need to think about the composition. In fact, many people claim that photography is not about having expensive equipment and high definition photos at all. Even the cheapest point and shoot camera or a smartphone can take a great photo. The photography is all about the photographer's eye. It is about the photographer's interpretation and representation of the world around us. That is why there are so many branches of photography: sport, product, fashion, journalism, art, landscape, portrait, and so on.

All these branches are not set in their own rules. They constantly intermingle and build on each other. A good photographer is capable of combining the elements of landscape photography with sport, or fashion with product fine art photography in order to get unique photos that will capture the attention of the observers. A good photo is composed just as a good piece of music is. That is why combining the elements of photography is called composition in the first place. A photographer is composing the image that he sees. He observes, assesses, and makes conscious decisions about all of the elements which will make up a photo. Even the editing process is part of the composition, and that is where lots of the magic comes from.

Composition

Composition is crucial for photography because it can make an amazing image or it can make it awful. If you see an interesting object, it is not enough to raise your camera and shoot it. You are the decision maker, and you have the power to make the photo awesome. Move forward or backward, and you are already changing the composition. Change the lens, try out a wide-angle, or try shooting from below or from above. See what works the best and what you like the most.

Keep in mind that just like in music, there are rules to composing a good photo. Many artists defend their mistakes by saying "rules are there to be broken," and although that is somewhat true, you can't break the rules you don't even know about in the first place. An expert eye will easily see through a mistake. Breaking the rules in art needs to be intentional and with a point. That intention and the point need to be clearly represented. Again, the expert eye will easily notice if the artist is breaking the rules with intention or if he is just masking a mistake.

You might ask yourself, why are rules necessary? Why can't artists have complete freedom? Isn't art supposed to represent what we see and how we feel? The simple answer is that as an artist, you need to have the audience in mind, especially if you want to become a professional photographer and earn some money. Often you will shoot commercial photos, and you will have to design them in such a way that the audience, or potential buyers, find them attractive. From thousands of years of expressing humanity's thoughts and emotions through art, we gain experience, and we can easily tell what people find attractive. The photography rules are very similar to painting rules because both are visual arts. Remember that at the beginning of this book we said that photography is often called "painting with light"? That is because it is true. A painter will use canvas and paints to paint what he sees, while a photographer will use the camera's sensor (or film if using an analog camera) and light.

Even though the rules exist in the composition of photos, they are not the most important principle. In fact, your intention is. You should strive to choose those rules that you can use to show your intention. Sometimes you will accidentally get a good photo, but nothing in photography should happen by accident. You need to be in full control and make the decision through which you will show exactly what you envisioned before shooting. As you get more experience, putting a conscious thought to your photos will become easier. In fact, it will become the most enjoyable process as that is when you get to be the most creative. Photographers have a trained eye, and they are capable of making decisions in a split second. To get this training, the best thing you can do is go out and shoot, but think about every frame before you press the shutter button. See all of the elements and give it time to sink in. Then decide how you would like to compose the scene. Experiment and play. There is no better way to learn.

Elements of a Photo

The elements of a photo can be literally everything that you see in your photo. And that is not just objects, but their shape, colors, textures, lines, and so on. Of course, that doesn't mean that you should break down every object you are taking a photo of to its basic elements. You, as a photographer, have full control to decide what will be seen as an element. For example, if you are taking a photo of a glass filled with wine, it can be just that: a glass with some wine in it as an element. However, you can go further and notice the curves of the glass or the color of the liquid as separate elements, and then you can design the scene around them trying to emphasize those curves or colors (or even both).

Points and Lines

The most basic elements of a photo are points and lines. The **points** don't exist physically, but they are the spots in the frame where an object will be. You should consider the points to be the interesting places in the frame. It is where you want the observer to focus. A single photo can have one or more points of interest, depending on what story you are trying to tell. If you have one point of interest in the composition of a whole photo, it will probably be an object that will occupy a small to medium sized space. If you take a close up of a person, let's say a whole face, it will make the most of the space in the frame and it will have multiple points of interest. The observer will pay close attention to details such as eyes, nose, and mouth. Even if you take a close up photo of a simple object such as a clay pot, the observer's attention will be drawn to certain points where the texture creates an interesting pattern or where two different colors meet.

The majority of modern cameras have a grid that you can see through the viewfinder. Even the LCD screens have them. They look exactly like the grid for playing tic tac toe. This grid is there to help you compose your images. The meeting points of the lines are common points of interests. The empty space between the lines serves the same purpose, and so do lines. They don't have to be used at the same time; they are there to help you position the subject you are shooting in a creative way that will draw the observer's attention.

Keep in mind that different groups of people have different senses of aesthetics. People in the western hemisphere tend to read from left to right. For centuries, our eye has been trained to move from left to right. Even when we are reading human expressions, we tend to look at the left side of peoples faces first, and then move to the right. Because we developed this habit, the western audience will prefer a photo which displays the point of the interest to the right. High contrast usually grasps the observers' attention first. If you place a high contrast subject to the left, your composition will be successful. Of course, there are exemptions from this rule, and you should not constantly strive to achieve it. Sometimes placing the object to the right will have a stronger effect, especially if you are trying to alarm the audience or express strong emotion.

While points are places of interest on the photograph and they don't really exist as objects, **lines** can be both real and imaginary. Lines are often referred to as "leading lines" because that is what their job is. They will lead the observer's eye and attention from one point of interest to another. The existing lines are, for example, physical objects such as telephone lines, railroads, or a street. The imaginary lines are implied. They do not exist physically, but you still follow them. It is an imagined line that leads towards the direction the person in the photo is looking at. If there is a thing in the photo that draws your attention from one point of interest to another, remember that in between them is an implied line.

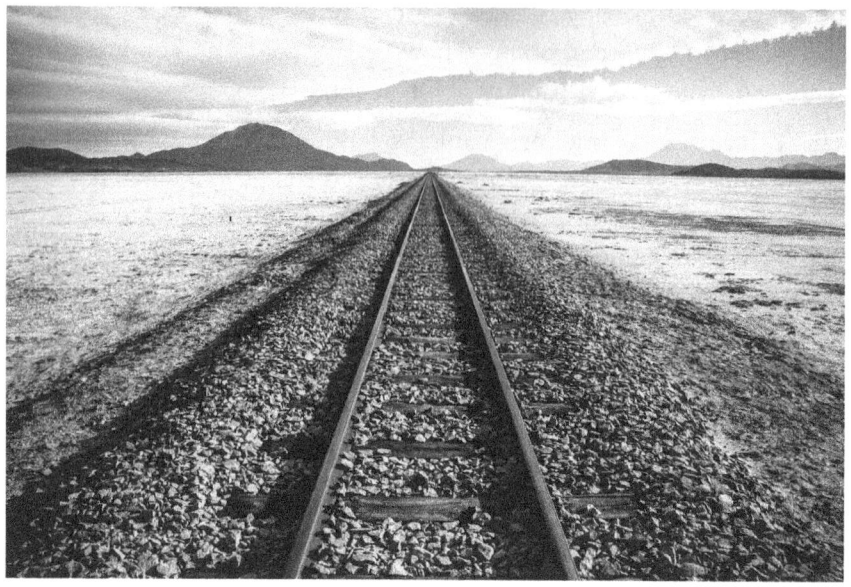

(Photo 7. The railroad acts as the leading line. The observer will most often start looking at the bottom of the photo and follow the railroad to observe the vastness in the distance.)

The Rule of Thirds

The rule of thirds is the most common and used composition principle out there. This is simply because it works! People love photos (and paintings) that follow this rule simply because they are aesthetically pleasing and they grab attention by moving the point of interest from the center. In the previous section, we talked about a photographic grid and how it can help you compose your photos. This is where that grid becomes extremely useful (two horizontal and two vertical lines which create 9 boxes). It divides the frame into thirds, horizontally and vertically. Remember that the rule of thirds can work in all directions. You need to place your object either to the right, to the left, to the top or the bottom. Rule of thirds means your main subject needs to occupy one-third of a photo, leaving the other two thirds empty (or occupied with objects which are less important).

When you imagine the photo grid or look through your viewfinder while turning on the option for the photo grid, you will notice the points where the lines intersect. There are four places where the lines meet, and they are called the "golden points." They have the highest visual impact, and your main subject or point of interest should be placed on one of them. But this doesn't mean you should always strive to use the golden points, sometimes missing them can have a stronger effect. Experiment and see what suits the frame you imagined.

Many beginner photographers have a hard time breaking away from positioning their main subject in the center. But the rule of thirds is exactly what separates a good photo from an average one. Of course, this doesn't mean that all photos who follow the rule of thirds are good or that those with the subject in the center are all bad. It simply means that by carefully planning where you will put the main subject, you can create an interesting and dramatic effect that will attract the observers.

We already said that western world has a habit of noticing things on their left side first, and then they move to the right. By following this simple rule, you can grasp the attention of your audience. The rule is something already familiar to them, and they will be attracted to it. However, you can also choose to put your subject to the bottom or right side, and this can have an even stronger effect. People will be taken with the uncommon design, and they will be curious to see it.

It all comes down to the idea of the emotion you want to stir in people. If you are looking to create a calming photo, which would inspire positive and warm emotions, you would place your subject to the left. People tend to find comfort in familiarity, and warm emotions are stirred when the design is already known to them. It is like coming home from a long trip. On the other hand, if you want to display something dramatic and shock the audience, you will place it anywhere else in the photo (except the center and the left side). If you are photographing a subject that is broken or in turmoil, by placing it to the bottom or top of the grid, you will draw the audience's attention quicker. The unfamiliarity will make them feel mildly uncomfortable but curious.

Rule of thirds is very simple when it comes to portraits. If a person is looking to the right, you want to place him on the left third of the grid. If he is looking to the left, place him to the right. This is because a person is looking at something (not really, but that's the impression), and even though we cannot see what he is looking at, we tend to follow his gaze. Even if there is nothing to be seen, we feel comfortable knowing there is a space between his eyes and the imaginary object he is looking at. Of course, this rule can be broken for dramatic effect, especially if there is something behind your subject that you also want to include in the photo.

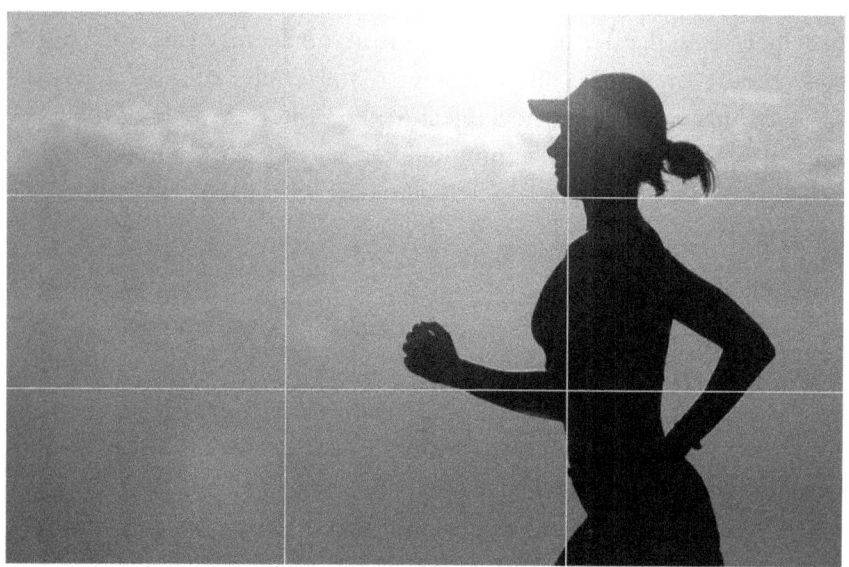

(Photo 8. Example of the rule of thirds. You will notice that the subject is placed to the right of the frame. This is done intentionally, as she is running towards the left. The left side of the photo is empty, thus enhancing the impression of movement, and the fact that the subject is running toward something.)

Foreground, Background, and Space Between

All scenes have three main parts: foreground, background, and midground. Working together, these three elements give a photo the feeling of depth, the illusion of three dimensions. In essence, these three elements are what creates a sense of space. Your subject can occupy the space of the foreground or midground. However, in special cases, it can even be in the background. (Think of the distant mountains as a subject of a wide landscape photo.) The easy way to make your subject stand out and grasp the attention of the viewers is by placing it in the foreground because this position will maximize the size of the subject and make it important, and the viewers will be immediately drawn to it. However, a subject in the foreground is not a dynamic one nor does the photo as a whole give the impression of depth. To achieve this, you should strive to place your subject in the midground or background. Look back at the photo of a rabbit in Chapter 2. The main subject is placed in the midground, allowing the sense of depth through the use of blurred foreground and background. The smart use of aperture setting will help you achieve this look very easily.

Beginner photographers often ignore the background and think that because it is behind the main subject, it has no importance. But this is wrong. The background is capable not just of emphasizing the subject; it can also tell a story when composed in such a way to make a whole with all the elements of a photo. Even a blank negative space for a background can leave the impression of vastness or emptiness, evoking various feelings in the observer. If you want the background to help the subject stand out, it doesn't necessarily mean that it has to be blank and without interest. It can support the main subject by contrast, texture, or lines that can lead the viewers' eye to the main subject. Remember that background is very important. It supports the main subject, and it can tell the story of the whole photo.

If you use a wide-open aperture, you will get blurred background and foreground. This will help the illusion of three-dimensional space, but you can also use the foreground creatively. The blurred elements in the foreground can frame your subject, making it stand out even more. However, empty space in the foreground also needs to have a purpose, and by forcing it to achieve a sense of depth, you are falling into the trap of taking bad photos. Use foreground to show the space, if the composition demands it. Don't force it. Or emphasize the subject with symmetrical framing with blurred out foreground, but don't strive to put just about anything in the foreground to make a point.

When you are combining lines with your foreground, midground, and background, take note of how they flow through the photo as a whole. Horizontal lines (where the sky meets the earth or the shoreline in the distance) will usually occupy the background. Make sure it is straight; otherwise it will create an effect of the whole scene leaking to one side. If you are using a diagonal line (imagine a path running diagonally through the scene), try making it start in the lower corner and end in the upper corner, thus achieving a proper diagonal line. This will give a sense of balance to the whole scene, and the viewer won't be confused with the position of the elements. Strive to find a perfect balance of elements that occupy all three grounds of a scene.

Simplicity or Chaos?

Photography is a form of art, and as such, it has a story to tell or a message to convey. Even product or commercial photography can and should make a point that it will bring to the customers. The story or a message can be expressed not just through the elements of the photo, but also through the way they interact (or don't) with each other. In conclusion, it's not all about showing the subject but also *how* you are showing it.

Composition can be simple or chaotic, and both types serve a certain purpose. The simple composition needs to point to exactly what you want the viewers to see, the main subject. There should be as few distractions as possible. However, this doesn't mean you should photograph a subject on a blank background. The simple composition can include various elements, but they need to support the main subject and emphasize it. Simplicity is a good type of composition when you want to make sure the viewer is getting the message loud and clear. With its neatness and familiarity, the simple composition will bring out positive emotions and a sense of calm. However, you can use a simple composition to show exactly the opposite. It is what strict minimalistic photography often used. Let's see it using an example.

Composition

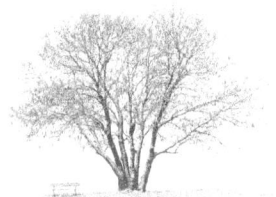

Photo 9. This photo is very simple with few elements. It is minimalist and familiar. But the scene and the position of the elements evoke the feelings of cold, loneliness, abandonment, and perhaps even death. It is a nostalgic photo evoking the familiarity, but it also conveys the message that all things come to an end.

Simplicity doesn't necessarily mean minimalism. Imagine shooting a performer, a dancer who is enjoying what he is doing. Instead of shooting the dance itself, try zooming in on his face to show the emotion he is expressing. Take a close up photo that will be filled with the elements (eyes, mouth, nose, skin texture, lines, and pores) but it will still be simple and in balance.

The opposite of simplicity is chaos. You can use chaos very creatively, although it can be tricky combining the chaotic elements in such a way to tell the story or to pass on a message. Chaotic scenes are perfect for grabbing the attention of the viewer instantly. He may not see the story behind the scene at first, but he will intentionally try to. Chaos composition is good when you want to make your audience think, for example, about some burning societal issues. The more elements, the greater the chaos! However, this doesn't mean that the elements should be out of balance or have no common interest points. If you are trying to convey the message that everyone had fun at the concert, you might want to take a shot of the crowd jumping, singing, and having fun. Static audiences won't say they are having a blast.

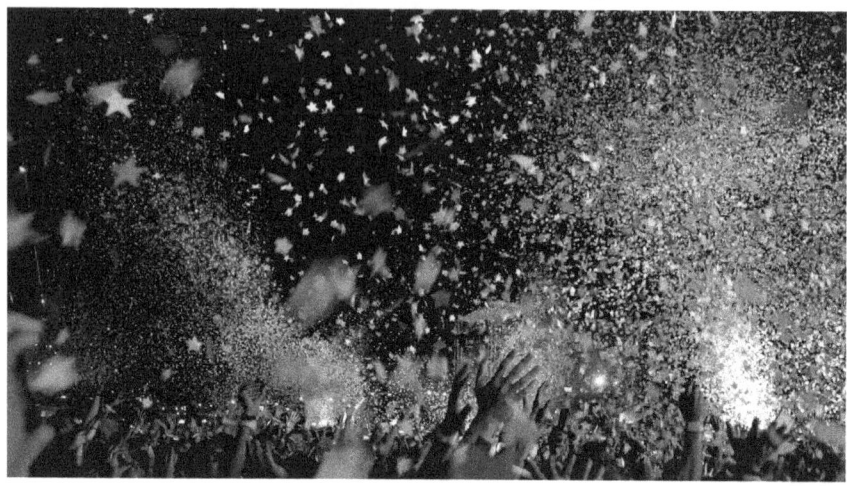

(Photo 10. Example of a chaotic photo. The colors of the confetti, together with raised hands, scream fun!)

Tips and Tricks for Better Composition

1. When you are shooting portraits, keep the focus point on the eye of your subject. However, not just any eye. If the subject is half-turned or turned completely to the side, focus on the eye that is closer to the camera.

2. To properly measure the light when you are shooting the portraits, half-press the shutter button while focusing on the skin just under the eye of your subject. However, if the light is not evenly covering the subject, measure it on the lightest part of the skin, set the exposure, and without adjusting it, focus on the eye before shooting. This way the lightest part of the photo won't be overexposed, but you can always lift the shadows to uncover the dark parts. This is done because post-process editing exposure on the whitest areas can lead to unwanted gray tones.

3. Avoid using wide-angle lenses for close-up photography. They will distort the face of the subject making it look odd. The photo will be unflattering and even comical. A wide-angle lens is good for portraits when you want to capture the environment around the subject.

4. Mind how you are cropping the body of a person you are shooting. A good photo will never end at the knees or at the elbows. The general rule is to cut just under or above the knees, wrists, and elbows. In other words, never cut at the joints. Don't forget to include people's feet in the photo. Beginners tend to forget about the feet or even their hands. It creates the wrong impression of amputation and the photo simply looks awkward.

5. The camera loves natural light, and you can always use it to get magnificent, natural-looking portraits with perfect skin tones. However, midday light can be too strong, and it will create very sharp shadows. Even though they might look interesting if you use props to purposefully make shadow patterns, sharp shadows are usually unflattering. Try shooting your subject when it's positioned next to the window. Curtains will diffuse the strong light and create a beautiful soft glow.

6. Avoid crooked horizon lines. It screams "beginner." Even if you take a crooked photo, don't be afraid to straighten it and crop it accordingly during post-processing.

7. Shoot horizontal for landscapes and vertical for portraits, but don't be afraid to experiment and do just the opposite. If framed well, the effect these photos create can be stunning. Remember to follow the rules, but also to playfully break them.

8. Remember that expensive gear is not necessary for a good photo. What makes it good is not its high definition and good quality of the image. It's the story behind it, the message you are trying to send, and the way you are doing it. Especially in the beginning, don't focus on the quality of your photos but on the rules and composition. You might even be surprised at

how good your photos are even with the cheap commercial camera or your smartphone.

9. When shooting children and pets, shoot with fast shutter speed to freeze their action. Our younglings are amazing in expressing their emotions honestly. Try to capture them to create a memorable moment. Pets are uncontrollable, and they cannot pose. Capture them in action while they are playing! You can even try the burst mode on your camera, and take several fast shots with just one press of the shutter button.

10. If you are using your camera in an unconventional environment, protect your lens. If you are in a windy area, the glass can be damaged by the debris blown your way. This is especially important if you are shooting in the desert or dry areas in general. Dust and sand can get into various parts of the camera and break it. The lens can get scratches of such magnitude they will be useless. You can protect your lens with a clear UV filter. It won't distort the photos in any way, but it will keep your lens protected.

11. Go to local galleries and observe other people's work. See what they are doing to be recognized as professionals and what makes them famous. You don't have to limit yourself to photo galleries. Visit museums and art galleries, and draw inspiration from famous painters of our past and present. Painters have magnificent talent to capture the light and various poses in their work. You can even try to imitate them for the sake of practice, but don't try to plagiarize them. Credit them whenever possible, and thank them for the inspiration.

CONCLUSION

In the modern world where nothing is permanent and everything is constantly on the move, it is important to capture the moments that we want to have with us at all times. It can be weddings, concerts, a night out with friends, or even protests, political speeches, or conflicts. There are various types of photography, and it is common for people to specialize in only one or two. But whatever you choose to shoot, there are the same rules to be followed in order to create quality well-defined photos with a story and aesthetics. This book holds the knowledge and information you need to achieve all that. However, there is only one way to get the experience. Go out and shoot!

It sounds like one of the cliché phrases that everyone is repeating, but it's because it is true. The whole knowledge of photography will not help you unless you practice and see the results for yourself. Get to know your camera and make it an extension of your hand. Try not to go out without it at all, as you never know when a good story is waiting behind the next corner.

One last piece of advice: don't be afraid to experiment! There are so many different ways to create beautiful photos, and you will discover some of them on your own. Once you fall in love with photography, there is no going back. You will start seeing the world around you in frames, and you will unconsciously make composition decisions. Photography is addictive. From time to time, you will catch yourself thinking "I wonder what that would look like through a 20 mm lens" and that's the moment you will realize you are hooked!

REFERENCES

All images obtained from Pixabay.com.

American National Standards Institute, and National Association of Photographic Manufacturers, Inc. *American National Standard for Photography (Optics): Camera Lenses: Focusing and Distance Scale Markings.* New York, N.Y., American National Standards Institute, 1988.

Collingwood, R G. *The Principles of Art.* Mansfield Centre, Ct, Martino Publishing, 2014.

Hammond, Arthur. *Pictorial Composition in Photography.* Nabu Press, 2010.